THE CRACKER
AND
OTHER EPIC POEMS

BY S.E. MCKENZIE

DEDICATION
To everyone who has been left out in the cold

THIS BOOK IS A BOOK OF SPECULATIVE FICTION
Characters, companies, governments, places, events, are either products of the author's imagination or used fictitiously. Any resemblance to persons (living or dead), companies, governments, places and/or events, is a coincidence and unintentional.

TABLE OF CONTENTS

THE CRACKER

CRACKER
I
Cracker cracking his whip
He owns the ship
He is in charge of your life's trip;

Don't give him any lip;
And don't feel at ease
His Negativity is like a disease

So hard to please;
As he puts up the wall
He wants it all

And he carries the keys,
To your door;
Rebel against evil for evermore;

Rebel against Cracker's Negativity
That pushed you onto the floor;
His Negativity steals your time as he salivates;

He even owns your door.
Ghetto Queen with phone in hand
In her tight black jeans

Is so quick to accuse,
Whoever walks behind;
Slams door in face with a look so unkind.

Nouveau Gestapo will beckon to her command.
We are not supposed to be seen
No one cares where we have been,

They have been indoctrinated,
And shaped by power of the lie,
How could they care if we cry?

Or what we know;
It is all about the show;
And the social media glow.

Dialectic of fear;
Taking over;
Acts like she owns every public place.
Addict of hate, Cracker salivates as he delegates;

Discriminates; loves to make others squirm;
Loves treating others
Worse than a worm.

Impossible to please;
You will be begging
On your knees;

Everything fits to a T
He says "Look at the great me."
You will be crippled if you don't follow me.

Count the cost of your loss,
For Cracker is your cross boss.
No sweetness can grow in the Cracker's mind

For he is forever willfully blind;
Possessed by the product of being unkind
Processed when selling pain and degradation.

So quick to tear others apart; negative sensation;
His favorite sport is breaking your heart;
The Cracker is cruel, the Warhead his tool;

We are left behind,
Cracker would have it no other way;
He never listens to what others have to say.

The Cracker would own the air you breathe
If he only could;
Settles on breaking the minds

Of those beneath; in his social order;
He praises his new wall and himself;
Laughing in glee he says "hooray for me".

The Cracker demands that you give him
A submissive look
Because he is the one that has written the book.

To remember for eternity.
Know him to a T;
He will be watching you and me

He watches but cannot see
The people on the other side
Of the wall;

Not under his jurisdiction to control;
Though he will try
To buy their very soul.

II

The Warhead flew in the sky;
Over Cracker-town where everyone was getting by
The Warhead looked down on the pawns from the sky

As the Warhead cried out in pain;
"Don't wanna overkill
The underfed again.

Don't want to kill
Little babies in the night
I want to hold on to you

And make love until the morning light
Shines in your hair;
Smile at me, show you care.

Don't want to be Cracker's delegate to instigate more hate;
Oh how I wish the Cracker could overcome
The hate in his heart; don't want to be a tool for a fool;

Or be made to me mindless and cruel;

Cracker made me tear apart people who had a heart;
I see Cracker celebrating instead of elevating those
Worse off than he; benefits the Cracker so easily."

III

Slum landlord, how he loves to discriminate;
The mass devaluation makes him salivate;
Doesn't value you enough to co-operate;

Blocks his ears when you try to communicate;
No need to elevate; nothing you say will he validate;
Won't fix the roof; teaches our young how to hate;

Slum landlord won't fix anything at all
Slum Landlord is ghettoized too;
Will make you feel small and blue

As he lets all the paint peel
From the wall
The birds move into the hole in the hall.

Cracker addicted to negativity
He loves to salivate
When he preaches his Hate;

Cracker's followers
Are shaped with each word
Of indoctrination;

S.E. McKENZIE

What a sensation.

They chirp so happily;
They never had it so good;
This is the way it is

When the Crackers
Own
The neighborhood.

They put up the wall;
So they don't have to see us at all;
And if they do; they feel new age rage;

Lost conscience as they play
In the electronic
Killing field.

Everyone feels helpless; it is understood
Why evil pig farmer looked so good.
The wall grows higher every day;

So the gatekeepers to life
Have it all
Their way.

THE CRACKER And Other Poems

Cracker has engineered cruelty to a T
Always watching but cannot see
The value in me and you;

The opportunity cost;
What has been lost;
Behind the wall.

Trapped in Crackers assumption
A victim of his consumption;
Fall under his spell, you will lose your gumption

Cracker, addict of Negativity
That steals time from every day
Throwing his projection on you, his way.

In our pad as cold as stone.
For the Cracker controls the thermostat.
Degradation hurt sensation; ancient frame of mind

To make Cracker glow in glee when being unkind;

Process of dehumanization; a hurt sensation;
Process creates the problem; Our life is shorter
Than his; he turns us against each other

No longer sister and brother;
Cracker addicted to Negativity
Takes control of the thermostat

Cracker tells you when to be warm
When to be cold;
How to live and how to grow old.

When we look up into the sky
We feel so alive
Which is better than wanting to die.

Cracker upsets the heart for sport;
While we fall through the cracks; faulty process;
No redress; Cracker's addiction to negativity

Warps what is appropriate;
Makes him salivate
When he abuses power to discriminate.

Steals your life away.

Ghettoization
A new sensation
In this age that widens the gap

Between the haves and have nots
There is no cap;
Oh how the Cracker laugh

In the aftermath
As he grows richer; taking over
Without introduction;

Every day your value will be in reduction.

Sharing power
Is not what the Cracker will do;
He cracks the whip

With a sour face
And he soon will own
Everyplace.

Your roof will leak
As you feel meek
He will yell at you

As you try to speak;
But the birds
Living in the hole in the hall

Have never had it so good;
That is what it is like
When the Crackers

Own the neighborhood.

Hear him fight
Over the hot water bill
That was so unfairly divided;

The Cracker way.
Building so high
Until there is no space in the sky.

IV

New age of rage;
Too young to die;
Too old to give it another try;

Master class;
Smile
As you behave as a slave.

The Cracker will drive on by
The Revolving Door; before he comes to a stop;
He comes out and expects you to hop

At his bidding;
Refusing him is forbidden;
He carries a chain of keys;

To get along
You cannot speak
For Cracker will turn up the heat;

He is the master of the only reality now

He owns the doors
Of all the tenants in his block;
His callousness sends some into shock;

Poisoned and broken frame of mind;
Too hard to heal; the ghetto is now inside;
Now he is a victim of a world unkind;

So cruel when Cracker is willfully blind.

Can't reflect just neglect one side;
Murdering the other side;
The ultimate sum zero game called war;

Kicking the living
Onto the floor; push them through
The Revolving Door; this power

And all its glory; couldn't be a more gory story;
Rewritten in misrepresentation;
As the Cracker's vibes caused a negative sensation;

As Cracker walks in without a knock;
He owns the block;
Don't like it

Then live under a rock.
For the Cracker does not have to be kind;
He can bully who he wants as he carries all the keys;

You work as a slave for nothing at all
For the building is about to fall;
The Crackers walk by

How they laugh
As they make you cry;
As we get buried in the aftermath.

They don't even try
To communicate
To understand and to validate

Our value; Looks like a jailer
With all his keys;
He walks around proudly

He talks loudly;
About things that should have been private
Make him hate and salivate;

To get along
You must bow
Sometimes on your knees;

His Negativity
Spreads like a disease
Impossible to please;

You must hold on to the dream
Or your pain
Will make you scream

And to get along
You must not speak at all
Or be seen

Unless you want
The Cracker to get mean.
See how he breaks another person's mind;

As the victim goes into shock;
The cracker doesn't have to knock;
For the Cracker owns the entire block.

New world order

Colder than ever before;
New age of rage
We are kicked

Until we fall on the floor
Now we know
What we were fighting for.

Did we bend over backwards to get along
As barriers were put up
No one wanted us to hang around.

In the crackers world they didn't want to see us at all;
That was why they put up the wall;
As we starved, too weak to crawl

The new religion
Was written on the dollar bill;
In God we trust

While so much around us
Just turned to rust;
Poisoning the Earth's crust.

Disenfranchising
With a click of a phone;
Death sentence without a name;

We wondered about it all not knowing Cracker was to blame.
Did we bend over backwards enough
To get along?

Worked free like a slave;
And it still
Was not good enough.

Slandered by a click of the phone
By any mean girl who walks by
We are so hungry and cold

We could almost cry.

As Cracker slandered us
With self-fulfilling prophecies?
Did we bend over backwards enough?

What could have the world been
If it had more love?
As no entrance sign stunted progress for some

The watchers turned away
For they could not see
On the other side of the wall.

Yes, we were up against the wall;
There was no empathy for us
At all.

Cracker did not want to see us;
Did not want to hear us;
Or live near us.

That is why he put up the wall.

We lived in one of the coldest countries on Earth;
Many of us turned to ice;
And were officially called missing;

No one wanted us in plain view;
No one spoke to us al
Or said "how do you do?"

They wanted us behind the wall.

We found places
Where grass
Could never grow.

We were circled
By strings of the unexplained;
Not knowing how much we had gained.

As the Church Lady
And Grumpy Old Man
Yelled at us so rigidly;

Told us we were too stupid to understand
Had to follow their every command;
Or we would never know

How the real world works;
While Cracker had the keys;
We had our memories;

He turned the water
And Heat off;
And Church Lady said

Just close your eyes
And you will be saved
For soon you will be dead; lying in your grave.

And your Momma lacked skills";
The church lady shouted out loud
While the crowd turned around to stare

Church Lady said
That we did not know our own mind;
The new aggression;

Negative suggestion;
Condescending
Without bending

Sell it as healing
Without a feeling;
Have us kneeling

With eyes closed in prayer
As if the crowd
Was not there;

How they laughed;
They did not care
Who we could have been

If the world had been fair.
We knew to not swallow their pill
Process of overkill the underfed;

That made others so ill and many dead
Just for Gestapo's thrill he said our pain
Was just in our head; Zombified

Part of them died while the church lady lied;
Some thought they had a friend to hold on to
In the end everyone turned away;

Had nothing nice to say;
No one would answer the phone;
Left us all alone;

If we did not do exactly what they said;
Which would make our head
Dead;

Zombified; Hurt sensation;
Degradation;
State paid medication;

We were the sold out generation;
As the bulldozer surrounded
What was left.

Ready to pave the way
For a brand new
Super highway.

We were trying to figure out what to do
But everyone
Got in the way;

Gave us no say;
While Ghetto Queen
In her tight black jeans

Gave us the usual look of hate;
Ask us if we were following her
Into town;

We did not know what to say
Too many negative emotions
Got in the way

Degradation;
Our hurt sensation
For were we the sold out generation.

As Church Lady sent the viscous rumor
By email; grew like a tumor
Soon all thought it was true;

And very few knew
Who we could have been
If given the chance;

Instead hate pierced our heart;
With one glance;
Tortured our mind;

While they looked
So willfully blind
They stomp as they dance;

On your face;
Throw you
All over the place;

Church Lady thumped us
With her Holy Book;
She gave us her holier than though look.

While the bulldozer came to Cracker-town
Started knocking
Our affordable housing down;

Church lady tried to sell us a lie;
That we would be welcome
In a real home in the sky when we die.

And we could feel our alienation
A hurt sensation
In this world of so much degradation

Zombified by State Medication;
We tried to get along
So we didn't say a thing;

While the bulldozers
Crushed everything
That we had.

Made us feel hopeless and bad;
The look on faces
Made us look mad.

And all could do
Was close our eyes in prayer
Wishing the world we knew

Was never there.

And then someone in the crowd
Screamed;
And we wish we had the life that our Momma had dreamed.

We knew the mob, so indoctrinated
Was being regulated; had been fed a lie
And that is why

They salivated as they hated;
The same lie that made us cry;
Sometimes made us want to die;

And made the Crackers rich.
The mass snob
Would be worse off than us.

When the string of the unexplained;
Brought chaos;
The real boss of loss.

Though we knew our Momma
Tried her best to let us live in dignity;
It was the dawn of World War Three.

We rose up again in pain;
With new power
The Magnetic Field gave us

The unexplained string to hold;
Now we had more power
Than Cracker's hoards of gold.

The Magnetic Feld glowed around us;
As the new world's gate
Opened to us; free from hate;

In the old world; greed
Created need;
And Cracker took it all;

Manufactured pain and degradation to sell;
Without a purpose, he made hell;
As we watched it all burn;

How he used to scream at us;
Tell us to relearn
Now it was his turn;

To feel the burn.

We had no time
To wait
For a turn;

Cracker told us to get along
Cracker told us we didn't belong
Cracker cracked his whip

Cracker demanded no lip;
Cracker did not need to be civil
For he owned it all

Happy to watch us crawl;
While he burned out our mind
With his slander so unkind;

Yes, in Cracker's world
There was nothing left for us
At all;

We were left
To die behind the wall
In one of the coldest lands on Earth;

No one cared about our worth.
They told us to get along;
They told us that we did not belong.

And we felt the majestic
Power of the unexplained string
The chaos which grew in everything;

We hung on to it real tight;
We hung on to it with all our might;
We had so much love to give;

Though many said we had no right to live
We still had
Our love to give;

Though we could not communicate;
There was too much hate
Controlling fate.

As the wall shook
It came tumbling down;
All around.

THE END

PULSE

PULSE
I

The Ghetto Queen
Expands her domain;
More for her to reign

Over; Never knowing Joe's name;
Her fear
Keeps Nouveau Gestapo near;

Cultural Genocide;
Destroying
The foundation inside;

Poison in a bottle;
Added to the mix;
Cultural Genocide; Economic Fix;

Her expertise
Cultural Genocide
She will put a label on you

Not caring if it is not true;
Now Joe has nowhere
To hide;

For Ghetto Queen
Has destroyed
His pride;

Now filled with self-doubt;
Joe can only shout
Feels so ill; Ghetto Queen's thrill;

Cultural Genocide;
Wrong side
Of the wire

I feel it inside me;
Inside you;
Your Pulse is rising.

II

The Ghetto Queen's glare
The Battle Stare
She does not care

How she imposes'
Her devaluation of Joe and others;
Never treating them as sisters and brothers.

Ghetto Queen can't play fair
For her Fear
Is owned

And the process
With no redress
Grabs cash fast.

Fear to buy
Fear to sell
Just another hell

For those
Who cannot tell
A foe from a friendly

The Battle Stare
Is always there
As she runs

Creating justification
And a new sensation
To trap those

Who are sucked in
By her magnetic glare
Her Battle Stare.

Waves rise with the tide.
Where can Joe hide?
The Ghetto Queen's world is never wide

Still wild;
We watch those trapped trying to fight
Her Magnetic Force;

The war, just another power grab;

As she imposes
Her devaluation
On others;

Never treating them
As sisters or brothers;
As she destroys Joe's self-identity

He will crumble inside;
Weapon of war;
Guarded by Nouveau Gestapo

She darts outside her web of fear;
Her fear is always near
Ready to pounce and ruin the day;

As Fear's magnetic field surrounds Joe;
He has lost before he could begin;
No self-identity; Joe can't win;

The process
Was all about cash.
While Joe's mind is in a state of regress.

III

And love for the common man
Could not grow
In Ghetto Queen's heart.

She imposes
In mega doses
Rupturing self-identity of others

Never treating them
As sisters and brothers;
Imposed will; not goodwill;

Seems like
Every generation
From before

Becomes Cannon Fodder
For those who rule;
Devalue others in a way so cruel

Just another tool for a fool;

While we lose ourselves in love;
Only the stars see the one
Fighting for his life

Lost in the storm
Just another boat wreck
No one wants to see

On their beach so fine
They don't have the time
To embrace Nature's rhyme.

IV

Just another Life
Pulsating; floating
Never able to stay

Looking for a home
In the usual way
While the bulldozers

Ghetto Queen
Stares out her window
So alone

Her fear
Leads to the vision
Only she can assume

As she imposes

Predator Class; her mind
Full of suspicion
She makes a decision

Then toxifies
Poor man Joe's will to live;
Human Condition;

She pulls; the only way she can;
For the Ghetto Queen
Owns her fear; magnetic field;

Her subject matter
Makes so many sadder
As she turns suspiciously

So many feel accused
And abused
Industry from Hell

Made
To buy
And sell

Ghetto Queen
Dirty fighter
Creates the dispossessed

S.E. McKENZIE

Her social privilege and order
Can only make her
Fear more;

She locks the door;
Of her mind;
Becomes unkind;

Baiting and hating
In a language of tongues
And forbidden to speak

Makes so many weak
But Nouveau Gestapo
Pretends to be strong;

With his hand on his gun
He holds it;
Until his fear is satisfied;

The Ghetto Queen
Assumed her bias;
just another member; predator class;

THE CRACKER And Other Poems

To her advantage;

Bury what they can
In the memory
Of yesterday;

Little magnets pull and push away;

Did you hear his cry
As Joe fought for his life
All alone on his boat?

Joe tried to float;
Fighting the pull of the deep sea
Of fear and suspicion

That very one; with waves
Of overpowering pull;
Into Time and Infinity;

Lost in the sea;
Of uncertainty;
Now Joe's world is upside down

While Ghetto Queen glees behind her frown
How she loves
Putting Joe down.

Holding his life
Was about to capsize
Overloaded with fear and lies

Of yesterday
Joe could only know
What he had left behind;

His life so harsh;
He could not be kind;
His hunger made him blind;

His hunger hurt so bad
He was about to lose his mind
While the Nouveau Gestapo

Stood by
While food was thrown away
He looked away

As the ghetto queen
Was wearing new attire
As she loved to hear.

V

Time heals;
Time kills;
And many kill time.

The beautiful voices
Sing in a Collective Choir
That Joe is excluded from;

He has his own song
With no one
To sing along.

The ageing elite will soon tire
And fade away.
Into memories that will inspire;

So much glory
So much not said;
When repeating the story.

Creation

Destruction
Magnets attract
By opposite poles.

The poles clash
We like magnets are pulled
Into the magnetic field

Now stuck
We cannot be free
Until the pull weakens.

While Time heals;
Time kills
And many kill time.

As the magnet pulls
There is nowhere to hide
From the force of Pull;

Power to buy and sell
Keeps us alive;
Expands possibilities;

Economies;
Feeding life
Difference between heaven and hell;

Who owns the means
Owns the story
Or so it seems

The beauty of the day
Takes my breath away;
And so quick to fade away

The moment cannot stay
But is now lost
In the emptiness

Of the past

This side of life's beauty;
I see
Is astounding

Leaves my heart pounding

S.E. McKENZIE

For I am alive
I will survive
To see another day

Just like today
Will fade way
Into tomorrow;

No one can see Joe;
All alone;
Clinging to what is left of his life;

Trapped in the magnetic pull;

Ghetto Queen's Battle Stare;
The Trumpet's Blare;
The Plague of Despair

So eager to share

Famine, war, disease and hunger
Were never meant to be;
For Paradise

Was never meant to be
As cold as
Ghetto Queen's eyes;

Joe clung to life
In all his misery
He still wanted more;

His thirst for life
Was easy to ignore
While the Ghetto Queen

Closed her door.

THE END

S.E. McKENZIE

THE PULL

THE PULL

I

Sam was pulled
Like a puppet
On a string; rose above the tide;

As the wind came in.

Drowning in the beauty
Surrounding the wall, guarding it was his duty
To survive; to stay alive, he had to be a hero;

He grew from Love; magnetic force from above;
Opposing hate
To balance Mega-rich man's toxic state;

Favorite game of Bully-man;
Was to torment Sam;
Bully-man wanted Beauty; he wanted it all

Mega-rich Man's occupation and situation
Was built on a stack of cards;
He was protected by thousands of guards

Some are now resting in graveyards.
You are what you sew; even though
Bully-man was about to fall;

False pride; envy in a land of plenty;
Never asking; always taking and faking;
Never knew if Mega-rich Man had lied.

Before he bought the massive wall;
For protection he said; the prison was in his head
Sam was never told;

The Gatekeeper from hell;
Would never tell
His true motivation;

When making a decision;
Offered help but then marked Sam like a beast
Big Boss; bigger Loss;

See how Mega-rich Man loves to feast;

Some pull;
Some push;
Not a word they speak;

Like a puppet on a string; holding on in the storm;
The dispossessed; victim of process;
Bully-men were always targeting the weak.

The Bully-men took it all;
Even though they are about to fall
After they finished building the wall.

For Mega-rich Man

Wanted everything
That money could buy
To hear Beauty sing

And to listen to his lie;
He even owned Ghetto Queen's Dress;
For he controlled almost every material process.

All Sam could do was reflect
As he awoke from the night;
He wanted to do everything right;

But beauty was in his sight;
He was pulled by Beauty's might;
Nowhere to belong;

He had to stay strong
For he was just another hero
Guarding the wall.

There was no real redress;
For infinity had no door
For those without physicality.

Sam rose above the tide;
Water circling; no need to hide
Sam has never lied.

Even though
Mega-rich Man
Tried to buy immortality

Immortality was just another lie.
What mattered
Was left behind

As Ghetto Queen put down her crown;
Without a word to speak;
How she praised the meek;

Needing something
To cling to; rising above the tides;
Conditions determine

Who Sam can be

Shaped by his drive to be free
Balanced by the moon and sun;
Holding on as the storm came in.

Out of bounds
Into a world
Beyond the wall

The climb was hard; once on top
Sam felt so tall
Above the wall

But beneath the wall
Many were hoarding it all.
They were expecting the fall;

Never questioned where the wall
Would crumble;
For the watchers watched but could not see

Behind the wall
There was someone else's space;
There was another stranger's face.

Clinging on
While the storm raged;
The only event that wasn't staged.

II
False Pride; only feelings they say;
Pre-judged to feed greed; nothing you can do, they say;
Greed created so much need;

Bully-man pushed into Sam
Sam was now possessed by Beauty;
Sneered as he apologized to Sam;

Smeared; as Bully-man lied;
Could not pull Sam's anger
From inside out

Or make Sam shout
Though Bully-man tried;
Grumpy old man beneath black hair dye;

Could never buy
Immortality
Though he tried; for he still believed the lie.

While Grumpy old man's anger grew;
For he knew;
His end would soon arrive;

He did all he could, and could not survive;
Once his hardened heart
Stopped pounding;

Would stay that way
For evermore;
In eternity; without a door

For those without physicality;
To prepare;
One had to change one's mentality;

Bully-man picked on another;
Closed his ears
While Beauty cried;

Bully-man smirked
With pleasure;
Only power he ever knew;

He had nothing better to do.
Than to dominate with hate;
Toxified fate hose with less;

Bully-man said he had nothing to confess.

While the watchers watched but could not see;
How his heart was losing the flow;
Soon Bully-man would have to go;

Into infinity; chaotic;
No dialogue;
Disconnected

Cannot relate
When in such a state
Could not hide

The power of his false pride
For evermore
For Infinity has no door

For those without physicality
There really is no
Immortality

It was all a lie
Though it was called truth;
As Bully-man's heart hardened

He hated anyone who still had youth.
And how his hate
Fed his fate while he ignored the truth;

For his greed
Kept so many in need;
Though he had no word

To speak out and shout.

He looked for the weak;
So he could pull out
Their anger to the surface

And hear them shout
In desperation
Hurt sensation;

Just feelings pulled from the inside out;
What a game;
To make those behind the wall

Cry and shout out;
'We are dying and crying while you are lying,"
Nothing new at all.

III

As the big machines dig for oil and gas;
The owners and runners thought
The damage would pass;

How could the Earth not shake
During a man-made earthquake;
And how could the wall not fall?

It did, the wall came down
No longer a game;
For the wall could not stand;

Under false command
Even with a lot of guards
It was only built on a house of cards.

THE END

FRAMED

FRAMED

I
Framed; Blamed; Named
Then came the diagnosis
At two hundred dollars an hour

"One day Woody may go psychotic."
Doctor Joe Inc. said
As Mary Joe gasped;

There is something wrong

With Woody's head;
There is somewhere
He would rather be instead.

So don't talk to him any more
When you see him;
Run out of the door;

Mary Joe's face will turned into a sneer
Cause her heart
Felt so much fear;

After the diagnosis
Was put on the internet for all to see
Who would you rather be?

Someone who still had liberty
And a chance for True love
And a happy family

Someone who had a chance
For riches and glory
And a happy ending

To their story?

II
Woody wanted to be
In a place
Where only the sky was blue

A place where few hold a grudge
And even fewer
Judge.

For only peace of mind
Helps Woody feel free to be
More loving and kind;

While the watchers stay willfully blind;
We don't watch
What we shouldn't see

And we think that is the way
It always should be.
But Woody was now all alone;

His True Love wouldn't answer the phone;

So afraid of Woody's new diagnosis
At two hundred dollars an hour
Buried alive in a negative file;

At the bottom
Of Doctor Joe Inc.'s pile;
He left it there without a smile.

III
Now the diagnostic tool number five
Would dissect Woody alive;
Just another billing code

To frame a case;
Push Woody onto the road;
Make Woody feel like a toad.

A diagnosis was so easily made;
In less than an hour;
Without seeing Woody's face;

Woody felt so bad;
He felt so much despair;
He forgot to comb his hair;

He didn't want to be displaced
Or to be disgraced;
Then he sand out loud

Even though it wasn't allowed.

IV
Woody was unwanted as a child
Grew up a little bit wild
He was often sad

Had no clothes to fit;
Was always afraid
Of getting hit.

It had always been that way
Never expecting love to stay.
He felt like a stray;

Then one day
He found a guitar
That had been thrown away;

Looked like the guitar;
Had been in a war;
Woody had never seen a guitar

So beat up before.

Woody looked around to see
If there was a trap set up
Nearby

Then his soul took over
And he started to rap;
Then put old guitar on his lap;

And drifted off
Into a nap;
Then he started to sing;

About what he wished he had;
And how much True love
When found would add magic to his sound.

Woody's voice was so sweet;
He soon was given enough food to eat
And a room to call his own;

He thought;
But it came to not;
His dream would be shot.

He signed the lease anyway;
He signed it in the usual way;
He felt so pleased;

Thought his true love might come back
Even though all he had was a shack
And was still living

On the wrong side of the track;

Then the rich man gave him his book of rules;
And chain-sawed through his ceiling
Turning his world upside down

The ceiling was now the floor
And Woody soon learned the score
How the rich get richer

And the poor accept their fate.
While the rich play dumb
While throwing a crumb

On the floor;
Bang the door
Before leaving like before.

No one was kind; they didn't have time;
Cause time was money
And nothing more;

And woody cried behind his door;
He cried harder than ever did before
While he started to thump the floor;

And then was left shaking
All alone behind his door;
Just like the way it was many times before.

He lied in his bed
His eyes were red
Cause he cried a lot;

At times he wished that he would get shot;

As the chainsaw went through his wall
He had no voice;
So he felt so small;

Then a Nouveau Gestapo accused Woody of using dope;
But Woody knew like we all do;
Dope is the Old Gestapo's rope;

Super fake;
Taking it
Is a huge mistake;

Woody was outraged;
Beyond his age;
He wanted a place to call his own

And he was so sad cause he was all alone;
In a hole
With a hole in the ceiling

And the wall;

He wished on a rap
Then he took a nap
Only escape from all the crap;

Woody just wanted a safe place for his head
To rest
It didn't have to be the best

Place in the world

Then Woody sang a song
And a producer came along
With visions of a money tree

He said "Woody let us make a deal
But you must play by my rules;
Your songs have such a great feel;

Could grow a money tree;
Spreading Hope across the land
Into Society and Infinity;

Growing a chance to escape
That hole in the wall
Otherwise could be your fate;

And your voice has so much power
It should be heard
You won't have to live like a sheep

In the herd'

Look at what was done;
Your life was turned upside down
Your power; it was next to none;

You are so young
You should have fun
But you have nowhere you can run to;

You are all alone;
you just have you;
But Woody you have a heart of gold

You will write songs
That will never grow old;
Maybe have a chance to really live;

Or accept your fate;
Such a sad state;
Left all alone;

As your heart turns to stone;
Stuck in that hole in the wall
Owned by a millionaire

Who will never care."

And then he said'
"Don't be too ready to die
In the war that is raging

Oil is over supplied
And Peace and Love
Are things money can't buy

So why would they
Give them a try?
Coffee could cost more than oil

If something isn't done
To decrease supply;
Could make many cry."

Woody went to work
All day and toiled
Came back home to see

A pipe
Above sunlight
Bursting from the sky

Into his ceiling;
He did not know
What to call the feeling;

That took over his mind and heart;
So he sang a song;
And his new found guitar played along;

Energy crisis
While the heartless machines
Dug holes so deep

For those machines never had to sleep.

Legislated poverty;
Trapped some all alone
So no one can see

But Woody knew

What it was like
To have to take
In so much crap.

Just another Millionaire
Who couldn't care
Turned Woody's world

Upside down

Now the glass ceiling
Has become the floor
While Doctor Joe Inc.

Tried to push Woody
Through
The revolving door

THE END

LIGHT

LIGHT

I
Light so bright
Could shine
In the darkest night

On Earth
So much fright
Decay shows its might

While God seems to be out of sight

So it is up to us to transform;
Go beyond the norm
Find shelter in the storm,

To survive
Trouble will grow bigger if we fight
Nature's light must win

Nature; the power to begin
Electricity
Super charged

II

Oh ancient power
More than just
Mysterious gas;

Sun in the sky
Without you
We would all die;

No one left
To cry
Or ask why.

Without you
Matter would have no life
And life would have no matter;

Without light
What would be sadder?
Without the glory; what could we believe in?

Where would we begin?

The light; we could never touch
So mighty and hot
Blinding to the eyes

When we stare;
So much to share;
If we dare.

Shine through
Humanity's disguise.
Sometimes without hurting the eyes.

Light does not struggle for power
For it is power
And only it can grant true power

To see in front of your feet;
Others will try to delete you;
With light's power they can't defeat you.

Light; we never get enough
Life; tries not to die
In this world of hate and decay;

Life would have it no other way;
If life could stay
And never decay

Would sad man
Rage
As age withers him slowly?

What if Nature had made him less lowly?

Grumpy old man
Hurts those below
Those he wants to know; hurts them if he can.

Tells them to stay polite
All night;
Forbids them to say a word;

So they stay out sight; It is his Watcher Job
To not see; individuals
Just the mob.

Know peace is collective;
Love can only be suggestive;
Crying alone in the night.

Light speeds through time
Curves and bends
In the circle of life;

And without the sun;
We would all die;
No one left to cry

Or ask why.

Feel it and you will never get enough;
Just like love
Softens with a gentle touch

Can hurt so much
When thrown about
Like the Lady with rose

She arose;
While the living were sleeping;
She looked over them while weeping

Holding a rose.
The light was creeping
Back into the sky;

And without the sun;
We would all die;
No one left

To ask why.

III
Reflect
In the world of neglect
So easy to forget

How we slow down
Decay
Day by day.

Sad man, angry man
Looks in the mirror
Every day

Hates growing grey
Hates fading away
So jealous of youth's beauty

He forgot his duty;
Though the sun was always there;
Didn't have to care to share its might;

Its light.

Life is round
And will always turn
So don't burn;

Out; Cycles circle
Into seasons of light;
Raging from the sky;

While Nouveau Gestapo won't hear
The other side cry;
So caught up

In their mind numbing Fear;

So afraid
To touch the ground;
Don't have to hear

Death rattle's sound.
Death comes as a shock;
It will never have to knock

Old man hides from death
Under his rock
But death takes him away anyway

Doesn't care
What he has to say
His life is now gone

Just faded away;
Too tangled up in his power;
He never expected death to call.

Life is too short
To fight;
But sad man does it anyway

To flex his might;
Before he loses his sight;
He hides his eyes from the light

He was promised a chance
To expand his life;
Though the promise was broken;

Earth's water veins
Feel so much pain
Clogged and hardened

The light shines anyway
For it must
Nothing about trust

Light was made that way;
Mighty power;
To defy decay.

IV

I walked on the street
Going my way
I saw the mighty power

Lighting the way
It gave me life
And time to reflect

Why did I ever
Leave my love
In neglect.

I held on
So desperately
There was no door open to me

My tears got in the way
And I just could not see
My true love was waiting

And was so close to me
But everything was different
There were so many new streets

That I did not know;
So many city lights
Shining too bright

The sky light
Was dimming
Even on the clearest of nights

I was too old now
To fight for my rights
I was still holding on

Desperately;
To the dream
That was so far out of sight,

I was losing my might
And I was losing my breath
I looked al around me

Property that I rented
But never would own
Been exploited all my life

But I never let my sadness show;
I played the game
So the thought police

Would never know
For so much was so selected
And so much was neglected

I was holding on to the time left
Seeing the light reflected from the sky
Never having really lived

And not ready to die;
I held on once more
To a locked door;

The Ghetto Queen
Looked at me
With all the hate in her eyes

But I was still able to see
Through her disguise
Knowing if I had been wealthy

I would have never been so despised

I held on to the dream;
And could not let go
I walked on the street

And saw places
That I would never belong
I felt so weak

But I had to be strong.
I was going home;
Where my true love would be;

I was going home;
What was left of me;
I was going home;

While the light shone on my path;
I felt no fright
Though I knew death would come to me

In the darkness of night.
I lived in the shadow;
That is what I know

I feel the light all around me;
I can feel it glow;
I see all the love

That had never died;
I see all the love still living
So I knew

That the Nouveau Gestapo
Had been lying
To you.

V
I am the sun
I give power
To all;

Strong and weak
New-born
Or lost in decay;

I am the sun;
Power that keeps life so warm
I am the sun;

Where there is no hope left
I will be the one
To shine;

I am the sun.

THE END

Produced by S.E. McKenzie Productions
First Print Edition 2016

Enquiries: 1(778)992-2453
Mailing Address:
S. E. McKenzie Productions
168 B 5th St.
Courtenay, BC
V9N 1J4

Email Address:
messidartha@aol.com

http://www.amazon.com/SarahMcKenzie/e/B00H9RWX48/

www.ingramcontent.com/pod-product-compliance
Lightning Source LLC
Chambersburg PA
CBHW070645030426
42337CB00020B/4165